# EXTREME CAREERS

# SECRET SERVICE AGENTS

## Life Protecting the President

## David Seidman

the rosen publishing group's
rosen
central

*To Marianne Young, who has helped to protect me from my own less-than-presidential dangers*

Published in 2003 by The Rosen Publishing Group, Inc.
29 East 21st Street, New York, NY 10010

Copyright © 2003 by The Rosen Publishing Group, Inc.

First Edition

**Library of Congress Cataloging-in-Publication Data**

Seidman, David.
Secret Service Agents: life protecting the president / David Seidman.— 1st ed.
p. cm. — (Extreme careers)
Includes bibliographical references and index.
Summary: Discusses the history of the need to provide protection for the president of the United States and describes the duties of the members of the Secret Service who fill this role.
ISBN 0-8239-3636-8 (lib. bdg.)
1. United States—Secret Service—Juvenile literature. 2. Presidents—Protection—United States—Juvenile literature. [1. United States—Secret Service.] I. Title. II. Series.
HV8144.S43 S45 2002
363.28—dc21

2001007486

Manufactured in the United States of America

# Contents

# On the Go

When terrorists attacked the United States on September 11, 2001, Japanese politician Takeshi Kondo was in Washington, D.C., waiting to visit economic adviser Lawrence Lindsey at the White House. "Secret Service agents came rushing into the waiting room and told us that a number of suspicious planes had entered prohibited airspace," Kondo told the Japanese newspaper the *Asahi Shimbun*. "They said, 'The planes are coming this way. There is no time to run outside,' and they escorted us to an underground conference room."

A few blocks away, in the United States Capitol, Laura Bush, the wife of President George W. Bush, was waiting to give a speech to a committee of

Secret Service agents with specially trained dogs make sure bags are free of explosives during a presidential excursion.

senators when Secret Service agents swept in and escorted her out of the building. They told everyone else to leave, too. Soon, all of the federal government's Washington buildings would be evacuated.

Meanwhile, Associated Press reporter Sonya Ross and other journalists were covering President Bush's visit to a second-grade class at Emma E. Booker Elementary School in Sarasota, Florida. Ross was bored until presidential Chief of Staff Andrew Card interrupted the visit to whisper in Bush's ear. The

A uniformed agent helps guard Air Force One on the tarmac at Barksdale Air Force Base in Louisiana just hours after the September 11, 2001, terrorist attacks.

president, his staff, and the journalists "sped from the school toward Air Force One," Ross wrote. "In a few frantic minutes, the Secret Service lined up everybody's bags, even those of [presidential] staffers, so they could be searched for the third time in as many hours."

After Air Force One headed skyward, Ross learned the details behind Card's whisper and the Secret Service's actions: Terrorists had crashed passenger jets into the Pentagon—America's military headquarters located near Washington, D.C.—and New York City's World Trade Center towers. The Secret Service's New York office, with 200 employees, was in the Trade Center; agents on Air Force One watched the plane's television screens in shock as the crashes triggered the collapse of the two towers and took out a large chunk of the Pentagon, killing thousands of people. Another plane was downed in rural Pennsylvania, though authorities believe that its hijackers had planned to crash it into the White House or the Capitol.

When a crisis hits the country during a president's travels, he usually returns to the White House. That's what President Bush wanted to do. "I don't want some tinhorn terrorist keeping the president of the

United States away from the nation's capital," he complained, but his Secret Service agents didn't want him in a city that seemed to be under attack.

But where should he go? The agents who rushed President Bush into Air Force One hadn't had time to pick a destination; they wanted only to fly him away from the dangerous East Coast. By the time they knew enough about the situation to pick a place to land, the plane was near Louisiana.

On advice from the agents, Air Force One touched down at Louisiana's Barksdale Air Force Base, where military jets could protect the president from attack. Within two days, the agents returned President Bush, safe and unharmed, to the nation's capital.

These events show the kind of actions that make the Secret Service famous.

# Life Under Pressure

The Secret Service protects the president, the vice president, and their immediate families, plus former presidents, their spouses, and their children under age sixteen. (The families' pets don't get official Secret Service protection, but they're usually near a member of the family who is under Secret Service protection.)

These agents also watch over important foreign visitors to the United States and major presidential and vice-presidential candidates and their spouses, but not necessarily their kids. To decide which candidates are "major" ones, the secretary of the Treasury consults with the leader of the House of Representatives' biggest political party (also known as the Speaker of the House or the majority leader), the leader of the House's second-biggest party (the minority leader), and the minority and majority leaders of the Senate.

"An attack can happen in milliseconds," Secret Service agent Larry McCallum told the *New York Times* during the 1996 presidential campaign. If anyone shoots at the president, agents will jump in front of him and take the bullet for him. "Every day is our Super Bowl," former Secret Service director Lewis Merletti said to the *Cleveland Plain Dealer.* "There's no, 'Well, we can afford to lose today and catch back up tomorrow.' There is no tomorrow . . . We need to win every game." No wonder Worthy of Trust and Confidence is the Secret Service's motto.

Then director of the Secret Service, Lewis Merletti *(center)* is shown in May 1998 leaving a federal court after a judge ruled that Secret Service agents could not refuse to testify regarding presidential matters.

It's also no wonder that agents feel constant pressure—not because they fear for their lives, but because they might let their guard down for a moment and an assassin could kill the president. In discussing his own career, former agent Dennis McCarthy has described the feeling as "like being coiled up inside a jack-in-the-box for sixteen years."

Regardless of the challenges of the job, the service has its advantages, too: Its agents travel the world, watch history being made, get to know presidents, and even get to tell them where to go and what to do. President Harry Truman said that the Secret Service was the only boss he had as president, except for Mrs. Truman.

What's more, for the agents, the entire Secret Service is a special family. "They see themselves as the best and the bravest of law enforcement," *Washington Post* journalist Peter Perl has written. "The Secret Service breeds a special camaraderie born of thousands of midnight shifts, of long weeks on the road together, of teams of agents planning and talking about how to keep the president alive, of new agents learning that there is a 'Secret Service way'—of acting, of speaking, of writing, of dressing. A certain way of standing quietly vigilant alongside the nation's leaders."

Former agent McCarthy may have put it best in an interview with the *Kansas City Star* when he said, "I'll never stop being a Secret Service agent. I think it's something you keep forever."

# On the Job

**1**

Secret Service sounds like the wrong name. How secret can it be when everyone has heard of it?

That's only one of the odd things about presidential protection.

## The First Guards

Early on, presidents didn't have much protection. They didn't even want it. Thomas Jefferson, elected in 1800, felt that keeping the public out of the White House was antidemocratic, so he opened the doors to everyone. The inauguration of President Andrew Jackson in 1829 would horrify today's

Secret Service: Thousands of people squeezed into the White House, putting Jackson in danger of being trampled to death.

When presidents did feel the need for protection—during the War of 1812, for example, when the British army invaded Washington—they used soldiers, policemen, or civilian guards. After a would-be killer named Richard Lawrence launched America's first presidential assassination attempt (he tried to shoot President Jackson in 1835), the government responded by putting a guardhouse and a sentry on the White House

This drawing depicts the first attempted presidential assassination in the United States: Richard Lawrence trying to shoot Andrew Jackson in 1835.

grounds. Presidents didn't have full-time bodyguards until President Franklin Pierce hired one in the 1850s.

# The Pinks: The Beginnings of America's Secret Service

The first Secret Service started with Allan Pinkerton, head of a company called Pinkerton's National Detective Agency. The Pinks (as they were called) guarded trains from theft, so the government hired them to guard Abraham Lincoln on a train trip to his presidential inauguration in March 1861.

When the Civil War began in mid-April, Lincoln's chief general, George McClellan, hired Pinkerton to set up a group of spies and secret agents. The government called them the Secret Service. Unfortunately, however, Pinkerton was a better detective than spy chief. He overestimated the enemy's power, which made McClellan hold back from battles that he could have won. The end of the war in 1865 saw the end of the first United States Secret Service.

At this time, states and banks could issue their own money, and they created a variety of different bills.

Anyone with a printing press could easily forge bills, called counterfeits, and claim that they were real. By the end of the Civil War, more than a third of the paper money in the United States was counterfeit.

The federal government's Treasury Department (the agency in charge of the nation's money) sent investigators to find and arrest the counterfeiters. On April 14, 1865, the day that John Wilkes Booth assassinated Lincoln, the president had signed an order making these investigators (who sometimes worked undercover) an official branch of the Treasury called the Secret Service.

# From Counterfeiters to Killers

Secret Service agents were so good at fighting forgers that Congress ordered them to find other crooks who were disobeying federal laws—for example, those who stole U.S. mail from postal workers or who took over land that the government had deeded to other people. The Secret Service had became something of a nineteenth-century version of today's FBI, the Federal Bureau of Investigation. (The FBI didn't exist at the time.) However, Congress never suggested that they protect presidents, even after mentally disturbed lawyer

# Secret Service Agents: Life Protecting the President

Charles Guiteau assassinated President James Garfield in 1881. In fact, only in 1894, when Congress investigated threats against President Grover Cleveland, did the Secret Service put agents around the president and his family—without Congress's approval.

The agents protected Cleveland only part-time and rather informally, but things changed in 1901 after Leon Czolgosz, a would-be anarchist (someone who wants to wipe out all government) shot and killed President William McKinley. Five years later, Congress passed a law that gave the secretary of the Treasury authority for "the protection of the person of the President of the United States." Ever since, the Secret Service has been in charge of guarding the president.

From time to time, Congress expanded the protection of the president and other dignitaries. In 1922, for instance, the White House police force was created to keep the executive mansion and its grounds safe. Eight years later, the force was made a part of the Secret Service. It has been known since 1977 as the Secret Service Uniformed Division.

In the 1960s, the Secret Service's job expanded again. In 1962, for example, the agency started

This 1881 political cartoon depicts Charles Julius Guiteau demanding a diplomatic post from President James Garfield, whom he later shot. Mortally wounded, Garfield died weeks later from the assassin's bullet.

guarding vice presidents. In 1968, after Jordanian immigrant Sirhan Sirhan killed presidential candidate Robert Kennedy, they began to protect candidates running for president and vice president.

Foreign officials came under Secret Service protection in the next decade. Since 1970, the Secret Service has been guarding foreign countries' Washington offices. In 1971, the agency began to guard foreign government leaders who visited the United States. And starting in 1975, agents have been guarding foreign offices in American cities outside of Washington.

In addition to expanding the range of people it protects, the Secret Service has expanded the range of people that it hires. In the 1970s, the agency accepted Phyllis Shantz, its first female agent.

Since the agents took on the job, thousands of people have threatened the Secret Service's protectees (the official name of the people whom the agency protects). There have been several murder attempts on the protectees, but only one has been killed: President John Kennedy, on November 22, 1963. Although it's the agency's only major failure, Kennedy's death haunts the Secret Service to this day.

# The Agency's Reach

The service has never quit chasing counterfeiters and other criminals who commit federal financial crimes. These days, its reach includes credit-card fraud, computer crime, and identity theft. (Identity theft involves using stolen or phony driver's licenses, credit cards, computer passwords, and other things to pass oneself off as another person in order to spend his or her money or commit crimes and get the other person blamed for

A Secret Service agent leaps (too late) to the rescue of President John F. Kennedy, who was assassinated on November 22, 1963.

them.) In addition, the agency takes on short-term projects, such as researching, in the wake of several shootings in schools during the late 1990s, why students commit murder.

The agency has field offices in every state and in cities from Bangkok, Thailand, to Berlin, Germany, to Bogotá, Colombia—more than 125 offices in all. Between its protective function and its financial function, the agency has about 5,000 employees. Like any other organization, it has clerks, secretaries, accountants, and office managers, but it also hires people with special skills. Chemists, electronics engineers, psychologists, photographers, fingerprint specialists, document analysts—the Secret Service uses them all.

# Agents and Officers

The Secret Service people you're most likely to see fall into two categories: special agents and uniformed officers. The service's 2,100 special agents are the ones in black suits and sunglasses who surround the president and other protectees. In addition, they investigate financial crimes and other Treasury

Department concerns. Like special agents, the uniformed officers (the service has over a thousand of them) watch over the president and other protectees, but they don't investigate financial crimes. Instead, they guard federal buildings like the White House and the Treasury Department headquarters, plus foreign embassies and other diplomatic buildings.

# Ways and Means

The agency's work is complicated, but it involves a short list of basic goals and tasks. Teamwork is vital. If the uniformed division can't get along with the special agents, if the Secret Service can't get help from the White House staff, or if law-enforcement agencies from the FBI to foreign police departments don't work well with the Secret Service, the result could be deadly.

Preparation is another important element in this work. When the president travels, Secret Service agents arrive at his destination well in advance in order to arrange every detail of his trip. When ensuring that a room is safe for the president to enter,

Among other security measures during a keynote address at the Republican National Convention by First Lady Barbara Bush, Secret Service agents confiscated newspapers to prevent their potential use in concealing weapons.

checking his food for poison, and watching for people toting guns, Secret Service agents work quietly so that no one will notice how they work and try to outwit them or get in their way. At home or overseas, agents try to imagine any potential danger to the president and design plans to keep him safe.

Another part of careful planning is attention to detail. In 1996, for instance, Secret Service agents took newspapers away from people who were waiting for First Lady Barbara Bush to give a speech. They were apparently trying to stop any would-be assassin from using a newspaper to hide a gun.

The best agents have an almost supernatural dedication to their work. Agents work almost one and a half times longer than most workers; they put in nearly 250 hours a month on the job, compared to the average person's 170 hours. Not only do agents work long, tiring hours, but they have to stay sharply alert for almost every minute of those hours. They know that at any minute, they could do something that saves the president's life—or fails to save it.

# The Way to the White House

*O*ne day you find yourself standing in the Rose Garden at the White House, guarding the president of the United States, and you say to yourself, "How did I get here?"

According to *Hispanic Times* magazine, that's a question that Special Agent Jaime Cagigas has asked himself. It's a good one. What kind of person becomes a Secret Service agent?

## The Protector's Personality

Top agents get described as low-key, straightforward, completely professional, and surprisingly friendly. But that's only part of the story.

Special Agent Larry Cockell, who led President Bill Clinton's security detail, keeps an eye on crowd members in 1997.

"We have a lot of Type A's and Type A-plus," agent Larry Cockell told the *Washington Post*. Type A personalities compete hard, love challenges, hate delays, and hurry to succeed at whatever they do. "We deal in an environment where critical thinking and initiative get high consideration," he says.

But Secret Service agents can't leap out impulsively with guns blazing. "You want people who are focused, mature, and disciplined," former special agent Jerry Parr, who guarded President Ronald Reagan, told the *Post*.

# Secret Service Agents: Life Protecting the President

Quite a few agents planned for the Secret Service at an early age. A number were kids or teenagers who were watching television in 1963 when assassin Lee Harvey Oswald shot President John Kennedy. When these kids saw agents scramble to save the president and his wife, they took the agents' heroism as their own goal. As Lewis Merletti has said to the *Cleveland Plain Dealer*, "When that all happened, that's when it hit me that I'd love to be a Secret Service agent."

Other future Secret Service agents prepared for their careers by studying criminal justice, political science, or other related fields in college, or by working as police officers or soldiers. Some hadn't given a thought to being Secret Service agents until they saw agents up close. Uniformed officer Oliver Hemsley, for instance, started as a White House messenger. On the job, he met a number of Secret Service agents and realized that he wanted to be one of them. Special Agent Kathleen Hickman, according to the *New York Times*, was managing a hotel in Dallas, Texas, when Ronald Reagan's Secret Service detail came by to work with her. (Reagan was planning to visit Dallas.) She liked their efficiency, and since they were recruiting women, she joined up.

# Time to Train

Once you qualify for the job, you have to go through training. The first stop is the Federal Law Enforcement Training Center in Glynco, Georgia, near the port city of Brunswick. The FLETC trains agents and officers for more than seventy federal departments as well as for cities, states, and international agencies.

Starting at the FLETC and moving on to the Secret Service training headquarters in Beltsville, Maryland, uniformed officers and special agents study criminal law,

## Getting the Job

To become a Secret Service Agent, you have to:

- Be a United States citizen
- Have a high school diploma or the equivalent
- Have a valid driver's license
- Be in excellent health and physical shape
- Pass a written exam, a personal interview, a lie detector test, a medical exam, a drug screening, and an eye exam (your eyesight must be no worse than 20/60 in each eye, and you should have glasses or contact lenses that correct it to a perfect 20/20)
- Pass a background check to prove that you're firmly loyal to the United States and won't reveal or misuse its secrets

physical protection and defense, police skills such as the proper way to conduct an investigation, and first aid and emergency medicine. In addition, special agents learn about counterfeiting and other financial crimes.

To be a special agent, you have to have all of the previously mentioned qualifications, plus a bachelor's degree from a college or university, three years of law-enforcement experience, or a combination of education and experience that's as good as the three years of experience and the college degree.

Beltsville in particular specializes in teaching the skills that a special agent will need most. A Beltsville trainee learns to spot and stop attackers, fire guns with laserlike accuracy, rescue a protectee from drowning, and drive at high speeds while making wild turns, even in bad weather. Training like this goes on for months, but it's not the end of an agent's schooling. "You typically begin by working in a field office to learn the different aspects of the job such as counterfeit currency investigations [and] cases that involve check forgery, credit card fraud, [and] computer fraud," Special Agent Jaime Cagigas told *Hispanic Times*.

A new agent spends seven to nine years in this way, sometimes working in widely scattered field offices. Eventually, the agent begins to get experi-ence in protecting people. But possibly the most important thing that he or she will learn is the Secret Service way to work: thorough, detail-oriented, secretive, and very efficient.

No matter how long an agent is on the job, he or she has to stay in top physical condition at all times. What's more, agents return to Beltsville for retraining every few weeks. They brush up on job skills, refresh their knowledge of law and other subjects, and learn new technologies and techniques.

# Ranks and Files

For fully trained and experienced agents, there is a wide variety of Secret Service jobs available. The fol-lowing is a sampling of the job opportunities:

- The Presidential Protective Division, the Vice Presidential Protective Division, and other divisions watch over the service's protectees.
- The Office of Government Liaison works with other parts of the government.
- The Office of Training supervises agent training.

The Secret Service must work with other law enforcement bodies, such as local police departments, the FBI, and the CIA, among others, to safeguard its protectees.

- The Technical Security Division, according to the Secret Service's Web site, "is responsible for providing a secure environment for all protectees at both permanent and temporary locations, and provides technical assistance to special agents on investigative assignments."
- The Forensic Services Division checks threats against the president by tracing papers, inks, and handwriting styles back to the people who use them.
- Counter Assault Teams are groups of sharpshooters,

In the wake of U.S. military strikes in Afghanistan in the fall of 2001, members of the Secret Service Counter Assault Team were dispatched to the roof of the White House to beef up presidential security.

positioned on rooftops and other places, who eye the crowd through binoculars when the president leaves the White House and stand ready to shoot anyone who tries to hurt the president.
• The Joint Operations Center monitors and coordinates the actions of the service's divisions.

Agents generally work in teams run by a special agent in charge (or SAIC, in Secret Service slang). Below the SAIC are supervisors who run squads charged with specific assignments like monitoring

The Secret Service's protectees include not only President George W. Bush but also members of his cabinet, such as Secretary of State Colin Powell *(left)* and Treasury Secretary Paul O'Neill.

lines of people who want to meet the president. And below each supervisor is his or her whip, or second-in-command.

Above the SAICs stand the director of the Secret Service and managers with titles like assistant director and deputy assistant director. Above them is the under-secretary of the Treasury for enforcement, and above the undersecretary is the secretary of the Treasury.

Finally, directing the secretary of the Treasury is a Secret Service protectee. In fact, it's the chief pro-tectee. Above the secretary, the undersecretary, the director of the Secret Service, and all of the agency's other employees is the president of the United States.

# Tools, Tricks, and Technology 3

**C**omputers and satellites, metal detectors and machine guns, bicycle patrols and armored "war wagons"—the Secret Service uses them all. Some of the agency's tools are as obvious as the fence that surrounds the White House grounds, or the compound, as the grounds are sometimes called. Agents on bicycles and on foot cover the compound, examining anyone who comes near. They look at everyone to see who's wearing and who is not wearing one of the special pins that the agency issues to everyone who works there.

Agents may search anyone and anything that enters the compound. In the early 1960s, agents stopped and questioned a Xerox salesman who was carrying bottles of something that looked like gunpowder. They released him once they saw that it was just copier toner, the powdered ink that copy machines use.

Even the president isn't free from searches. "For White House inhabitants, there is no such thing as personal mail—it is all screened," *Christian Science Monitor* reporter James Thurman has written. "Even the living quarters, including the sock drawers in private bureaus, are searched periodically for electronic listening devices."

# Dogs and Detectives

A good deal of searching is done by the K-9 division, which is composed of hardworking Belgian Malinois dogs and their human handlers. These amazing dogs sniff for bombs, drugs, and guns. July 2001, for instance, saw "the evacuation of parts of the White House and the Eisenhower Executive Office Building for about an hour . . . after a bomb-sniffing dog was attracted to a car parked in the driveway," the *New York Times* reported. (It was a false alarm.) At the end of the day, each dog goes home with its handler.

Other measures are more high-tech. Using metal detectors, which send out electronic signals sensitive to metals, agents scan for weapons on anyone who enters the White House. Inside the building, a web of motion detectors and other electronic sensors monitors activity. "Any little old thing can trigger that deal," President Bill Clinton told an audience of Secret Service agents in 2001. As a new president, he strolled from the White House's third floor to its second floor without knowing that he had accidentally triggered a silent alarm. "All hell breaks loose for the Secret Service . . . The SWAT [Special Weapons and Tactics] team occupies the staircase with their semiautomatic weapons. So they're all looking for somebody that's invading the White House. I come tromping down the staircase to the third floor; this [Secret Service] guy comes rushing up on the second floor. I look up, and there he is with his weapon pointed at me."

# Microphones and Earpieces

To alert each other as to who is wandering around the White House (or elsewhere), the Secret Service has set up some elaborate communications systems. Anyone who has looked closely has noticed agents whispering into their wrists. Agents are wired with microphones that transmit to tiny receivers in other agents' ears. The receiver is called, naturally, an earpiece.

# Techno-Tracking

To communicate over great distances, the agency uses satellites in orbit. These satellites also watch over any place that the president goes. As these

Secret Service agents, such as this one pictured using an earpiece, must employ sophisticated communications technology to stay connected to colleagues in tracking potential threats to protectees.

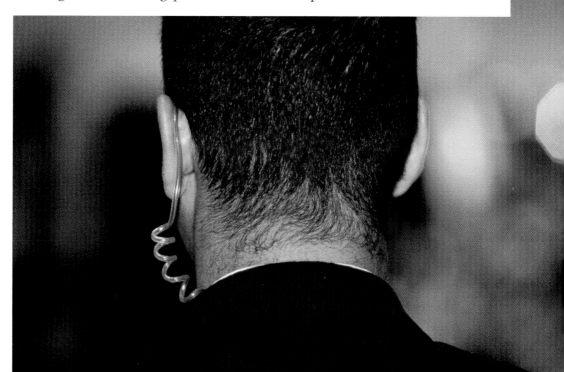

sources feed information to the Secret Service, the agency feeds it into its computers. If an agent needs to make sure that a White House job applicant is safe to hire, he or she can check computer files telling where the person has lived, whether or not he or she has ever been arrested, and other useful information.

The agency keeps a special eye on anyone who might hurt its protectees. It's against the law to threaten the president, and the Secret Service

Aside from agents in the field who gather information and physically defend the lives of their protectees, the Secret Service also has a huge staff who enter and analyze gathered information.

investigates every threat, no matter where it comes from. For instance:

- A New York state college student wrote a newspaper editorial that said, "Dear Jesus Christ, King of Kings, All I ask is that you smite George Bush," according to *Quill*, a magazine for journalists.
- A Toronto radio talk-show caller said, "We should do the United States a favor and kill [the president]," the *Toronto Sun* reported.
- A Detroit-area prison inmate wrote death threats to President Bill Clinton "because he is the ruler of the capitalist society," a Michigan state police detective told the *Detroit News*.
- And every fall, "some student somewhere thinks he's found a way to mask his identity online," *Toronto Star* reporter K. K. Campbell wrote in 1999. "So he gets online and sends off a mildly threatening 'anonymous' e-mail to the White House. 'And regardless of what trick they used,' says Professor David Jones of McMaster University in Hamilton, 'within 48 hours the U.S. Secret Service is in the kid's bedroom, pointing a gun at his head, saying, "Don't move," while they search the place.'"

An agent of the Secret Service watches over guests at an event in the White House Rose Garden in February 2001.

As if these methods aren't enough, the agency is always hunting for new ones. "Officials say they're developing stronger 'ballistic glass' [which can stop flying objects like bullets] and body armor that stops practically everything," *U.S. News & World Report* magazine announced in June 2001. "Even getting close to the prez will be tough for bad guys because the men in black are also producing facial recognition devices" to identify potential attackers.

Facial recognition devices, ballistic glass, computers, satellites, earpieces, microphones—these items are only a part of the Secret Service's toolkit. "There are many layers of protection, most of it not visible," according to Ron Kessler, author of the book *Inside the White House.* That invisibility helps to give the Secret Service its secrecy.

And while the Secret Service works hard at developing ways to protect the president in the White House, the agency gets doubly busy when he travels.

# On the Road  4

**W**e think of it as keeping the president in a mobile protective bubble," Secret Service agent Chip Smith told *New York Newsday* reporter Robert E. Kessler. He was referring to the challenges in keeping presidents safe when they leave the White House.

Presidents travel on their own planes and yachts, which the Secret Service checks for safety before the president goes aboard. The presidential plane, Air Force One, for instance, includes wiring that is shielded to protect it from an electromagnetic pulse, a form of nuclear radiation that interferes with electronic signals. The plane also has medical equipment and supplies to heal the president if he gets hurt. And Air Force One's ground crew travels with the plane so that no one but approved workers ever touch it.

# Cars and More Cars

Perhaps the most elaborate kind of presidential travel, though, is by automobile. The presidential car, driven by a Secret Service agent, is an armor-plated limousine accompanied by a motorcade of more than twenty other vehicles. They include police cars, an ambulance or paramedic vehicle, cars for the president's staff, cars for the press, and a decoy limousine to fool assassins away from attacking the president's

U.S. Army troops and Secret Service personnel unload limousines ahead of time that will serve as President George W. Bush's motorcade during an April 2001 visit to Quebec City for the Summit of the Americas.

car. Nearby is a Secret Service "war wagon," a mini-van containing heavy weapons plus a variety of electronic equipment to monitor everything that could harm the president. The Secret Service ships at least some of these vehicles wherever the president travels.

# Snooping Around and Taking Over

As previously mentioned, before the president goes anywhere, Secret Service agents get there days in advance to make sure that it's safe. Before President George W. Bush went to the Little League World Series in August 2001, nearly 100 Secret Service agents checked over every inch of the stadium. Prior to former president Bill Clinton's visit to a book festival in the English town of Hay-on-Wye earlier that year, agents investigated "all catering staff, the ice-cream salesman, and employees of a hardware shop opposite the site," said the *Times of London*. Special preparations were made before Presidents Bill Clinton, Gerald Ford, Jimmy Carter, and George H. W. Bush (the father of George W. Bush) visited the city of Amman, Jordan, for the funeral of Jordan's

The presidential motorcade for President Clinton during a visit with Russian president Boris Yeltsin in Moscow in June 2000

King Hussein. According to the *Washington Post*, Special Agent Reginald Moore "arranged for a secure, five-agent communications command post at the Marriott Amman, along with hotel rooms, cars, interpreters, street maps, emergency medical plans and evacuation routes, [and] security analysis of the motorcade and funeral procession."

These arrangements are hard on the places that presidents visit. Marion Lucas, president of the International Association of Fairs and Expositions, told the group's members, "Say no for as long as you can when asked if you want to host a president on your grounds."

The special arrangements aren't limited to the grounds. To keep anyone from ambushing the president, the Secret Service moves him by indirect routes. "Usually, when I go into a building, the Secret Service makes me go into an underground parking garage, past all the garbage, [and] up the service elevator," former president Clinton said. "The last time I went to the Hilton here [in Washington, D.C.], I have been in the service entrance so much that . . . they gave me a laminated [Hilton employee] I.D. card."

Travel by foreign leaders creates challenges of its own. When Pope John Paul II, Israeli prime minister Yitzhak Rabin, Egyptian president Hosni Mubarak, and other leaders visited Manhattan at the same time in 1995, the Secret Service organized what it described to *Newsweek* magazine as "the biggest security undertaking in history"—more than 3,000 federal agents and 5,000 New York City police officers. It worked. No dignitaries were hurt.

# Shaking Hands and Kissing Babies

Perhaps the kind of travel that Secret Service agents worry about most involves campaigning for the presidency. "Every four years, we have more work than we can handle," Special Agent Frank O'Donnell said to the *Los Angeles Times* during the 2000 presidential campaign. Protecting the president, the vice president, and all of the major presidential candidates and their spouses spreads the agency thin.

What complicates matters in terms of security is that campaigning politicians like to move among crowds and shake hands. "When people get that close, you can't see the hands of the ones in the back," one agent has said to the *New York Times*. "People are grabbing at the candidate, close enough for anything—a knife, [a] handgun, [or] throwing something." Agents often hold a president or candidate by the belt, hips, or waist, ready at any second to yank him out of a crowd.

Even after the campaign ends, the trouble goes on. A president's inauguration is crowded with dignitaries, ordinary people, protesters, and thousands of others— any of whom could cause trouble. When George W. Bush was to become president in 2001, Arthur Santana of the *Washington Post* reported, "Police officers will stand every six to eight feet along the inauguration parade route . . . [Agents and officers] will be watching everyone, from the air, from rooftops, from horseback, and from posts in the crowd." In case of a riot, "the Secret Service has a contingency plan for transportation, detention, and judicial processing of large groups of people." Agents even checked sewer manholes to make sure that no one hid there.

Secret Service agents don't discuss the subject, but they're no doubt relieved when an event is over, the visitors have left, and the president is safely back in the White House. They no longer have to worry as much about anyone popping the mobile protective bubble.

# Family Life 5

Whether they like a protectee or not, Secret Service agents must be polite. They also must stick as close to the protectee as possible. These responsibilities can make for some tough times. Presidents themselves recognize the problem. "You're impatient because you're tired and you've got a headache," Bill Clinton said about himself in a 1999 speech to Secret Service agents, "and you take it out by being a little short [with the Secret Service agents] . . . They have to put up with all of it."

When Harry Truman became president in 1945, his new agents didn't know he took daily walks, and they ran after him when he went out alone one morning. President Dwight Eisenhower had a farm overrun by groundhogs that dug holes in the pasture and under the walls of his barn; he asked his agents to shoot them.

# Forgetfulness and Friendship

Sometimes, protectees resent their agents' constant closeness and commands about what routes they can take and what moves they can make. On the other

President Harry S. Truman is trailed closely by his Secret Service escorts on the deck of a luxury liner.

## Teenage Trouble

Secret Service agents try to give presidential kids plenty of leeway. *Time* magazine reported that the agents around First Daughter Chelsea Clinton "cut her enough slack" so she could "manage a normal teenage life, like strolling with a date out of their earshot." But cutting slack can backfire. In 2001, for instance, agents let undercover police arrest President George W. Bush's teenage daughters, Jenna and Barbara, for underage drinking, much to the president's embarrassment.

hand, protectees may get so used to their agents that they forget about them. When President Richard Nixon was embroiled in the Watergate scandal, which eventually forced him to resign, "[he] sometimes liked to be taken on long drives around Washington," journalist James Carney wrote in *Time* magazine. "In the privacy of his limousine, he would discuss Watergate with his closet advisers. It never occurred to him to be concerned that his Secret Service bodyguard . . . heard everything from his perch in the front seat."

Though one former special agent in charge has said, "You want the president's respect but not his friendship," some presidents do get close to their agents. When attempted assassin John Hinckley shot President Ronald Reagan, agent Tim McCarthy leaped toward the president and took a bullet. Reagan was grateful to McCarthy, and he and his wife, Nancy, became friends with McCarthy and his family.

# Scorecard, Sawhorse, and Searchlight

While Secret Service agents keep their personal feelings about the president strictly private, the code names that they give presidents can partially reveal their honest opinions. Ronald Reagan, a former cowboy actor who liked to vacation on a California ranch, was called Rawhide. Dan Quayle, vice president under the first President Bush, got the name Scorecard, possibly because of his fondness for golf. Bill Clinton's vice president, Al Gore, was famous for his wooden speaking style and got the name Sawhorse, while scandal-prone presidential brother Roger Clinton was code-named Headache. Bill Clinton himself was Eagle, while George H. W. Bush was Timberwolf, Richard Nixon was Searchlight, and George W. Bush is Tumbler.

A Secret Service agent stands guard in front of
Republican presidential candidate George W. Bush and his wife,
Laura Bush, during an August 2000 campaign stop in Michigan.

No matter what they call their protectees, though, Secret Service agents will keep on taking care of them, even at the risk of their own lives.

# Secret, but Famous

"Building on a tradition of excellence and meeting the challenge of the future . . . the United States Secret Service protects our nation's leaders, visiting world leaders, national special security events, and the integrity of the nation's currency and financial systems." That's the agency's vision statement from the United States Secret Service Plan.

To reach those goals, the service intends to recruit new agent trainees, upgrade its technology, and increase its knowledge about dangers to protectees. It will frequently review and inspect its operations and workers. It will coordinate efforts with the FBI Joint Terrorism Task Forces, the Government Barrier User Group, the National Emergency Management Team, and more than thirty other organizations. It will do a lot of things that it will never reveal publicly.

And always, it will constantly strive to live up to its simple but meaningful motto: Worthy of Trust and Confidence.

# Glossary

**compound** An area surrounded by a gate or fence, with buildings inside.

**detail** A team of Secret Service agents.

**earpiece** A small transmitter that a Secret Service agent wears in his or her ear.

**field office** Any of the several dozen Secret Service offices apart from its Washington, D.C., headquarters.

**FLETC** The Federal Law Enforcement Training Center; it trains Secret Service agents and other law enforcers.

**guardhouse** A building, sometimes placed at the entrance to a compound, where guards are stationed.

**protectee** A person under Secret Service protection.

**SAIC**  Special agent in charge; a supervising agent who leads a team of special agents.

**sentry**  A guard who makes sure that only authorized people enter a building or compound.

**special agent**  A Secret Service agent who wears plain clothes rather than a uniform.

**supervisor**  A special agent who works directly under a SAIC.

**war wagon**  A minivan containing electronic equipment to monitor anything that might happen to the president, and heavy weapons to defend him.

**whip**  A special agent who is second-in-command to a supervisor.

# For More Information

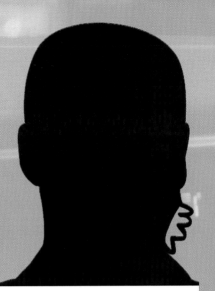

United States Secret Service
Personnel Division
950 H Street NW, Suite 912
Washington, DC 20001
(202) 406-5800
Web site: http://www.ustreas.gov/usss

## Web Sites

Due to the changing nature of Internet links, the Rosen Publishing Group, Inc., has developed an online list of Web sites related to the subject of this book. This site is updated regularly. Please use this link to access the list:

http://www.rosenlinks.com/eca/sese/

# For Further Reading

Cohen, Paul. *Careers in Law Enforcement and Security*. New York: Rosen Publishing Group, 1995.

Gaines, Ann Graham. *The U.S. Secret Service*. Philadelphia: Chelsea House, 2001.

McCarthy, Dennis V. N., and Philip W. Smith. *Protecting the President: The Inside Story of a Secret Service Agent*. New York: Morrow, 1985.

Motto, Carmine J. *In Crime's Way: A Generation of Secret Service Adventures*. Boca Raton, FL: CRC Press, 1999.

Rudman, Jack. *Secret Service Agent, Uniformed*. Syosset, NY: National Learning Corporation, 1994.

Venker, Marty, and George Rush. *Confessions of an Ex-Secret Service Agent: The Marty Venker Story*. New York: D.I. Fine, 1988.

# Bibliography

Carney, James. "The Boyguard: Shadows and Shields." *Time*, Vol. 152, No. 4, July 27, 1998, p. 22.

Clinton, Bill. "Remarks at the Dedication of the United States Secret Service Memorial Building." Weekly Compilation of Presidential Documents, California Digital Library, Vol. 35, No. 41, October 18, 1999, p. 2048.

Gaines, Ann Graham. *The U.S. Secret Service*. Philadelphia: Chelsea House, 2001.

"Junior Secret Service Manual." National Park Service Eisenhower National Historic Site. Retrieved September 2001 (http://www.nps.gov/eise).

Kalogerakis, George. "Protecting the President from Pizza: How the Secret Service Puts the 'Lid' on 'Eagle.'" *Vanity Fair*, August 1993, pp. 76–77.

# Index

## T

terrorist attacks of
September 11, 2001, 4–8
threats against president, 38–39
Treasury Department, 15, 20–21
Truman, President Harry S., 11, 50

## U

uniformed officers, 20–21, 27
United States Secret Service
Plan, 55

## W

White House, the, 12–14, 38,
39, 42, 49
fears about attack against
on September, 11, 2001,
4, 7
guarding, 14, 16
Secret Service and, 21, 31,
34–36

# About the Author

Other nonfiction by David Seidman: *Adam Sandler, All Gone: Things That Aren't There Anymore, Civil Rights, Exploring Careers in Journalism, Inside Stock Car Racing, The Longevity Sourcebook, Wonders of the World,* and *The Young Zillionaire's Guide to Supply and Demand.*

# Photo Credits

Cover, pp. 1, 5, 13, 17, 22, 37, 40, 46–47, 54 © Corbis; pp. 6, 10, 19, 25, 30, 31, 32, 38, 43, 51 © AP/World Wide Photos.

# Design

Les Kanturek

# Layout

Nelson Sá